Laws of the Bandit Queens

Laws of the Bandit Queens

Words to Live by from 35 of Today's Most Revolutionary Women

text and photographs by **Ali Smith**

THREE RIVERS PRESS / NEW YORK

Published by Three Rivers Press, New York, New York.
Member of the Crown Publishing Group.

Random House, Inc. New York, Toronto, London, Sydney, Auckland
www.randomhouse.com

THREE RIVERS PRESS is a registered trademark and the Three Rivers Press colophon is a trademark of Random House, Inc.

Printed in Singapore

Design by Elizabeth Van Itallie

Library of Congress Cataloging-in-Publication Data

Smith, Ali, 1969–
    Laws of the bandit queens: words to live by from 35 of today's most revolutionary women / by Ali Smith.—1st ed.
    1. Women social reformers—Biography. 2. Women Biography. I. Title
HQ1123 .S63 2002
305.4'092'273—dc21   2001027984
[B]

ISBN 0-609-80807-9

10 9 8 7 6 5 4 3 2 1

First Edition

This book is for Solveig Almaas, who deserves only the best.

And for my mom, who's given me her best.

And for my girlfriends, who are the best.

Contents

Foreword

My earliest female role model was my mother, a no-nonsense, no-holds-barred babe with biceps of steel. She and my father managed a stable, caring for some thirty-odd horses. I remember watching her push wheelbarrows, lift pails of water, and handle and ride extremely hotheaded horses. She was, to me, a fearless amazon. She spent her days in jeans and work boots with a crust of black dirt under her fingernails and cracks in the skin of her hands. At night, though, she'd shower and turn into a translucent beauty. And I loved this. That she could lift twice her body weight in horse manure and could, in theory at least, beat the crap out of most males but could also let down her hair, put on a dress, and turn heads from here to eternity. As my mother went on to become one of only a handful of female racehorse trainers on the East Coast, I grew up and—after brief stints as a horse groom, a go-go dancer, a maid, a nurse's aide, and a factory worker—turned into a writer who, thanks to some of history's most formidable women, has the freedom to do and say just about anything.

Over the years, I've become increasingly fascinated with the women who paved the way. I started collecting stories of suffragists and warriors, of women who'd gladly cut the head off any male but would fiercely protect women, children, and animals. I was both horrified and enchanted by the blood lust of nineteenth-century New York she-gangsters like Hellcat Maggie, who, tired of getting shoved around, filed her teeth to points and bit the hell out of anyone in her way. Then there was Sadie the Goat, whose MO was to sashay up to a man on the street, then abruptly tuck her head in and ram it into his stomach, stunning him so that her cohorts could spring on him and rob him. A large vixen known as Gallus Mag manned the bar at the Hole-in-the-Wall, a dive on Water Street. If someone displeased her, she'd bite off his ear, then preserve it in a jar of formaldehyde on the bar.

Around the same time, Victoria Woodhull, the first female presidential nominee, waged a more overt war for women's rights. Born in Ohio in 1838, she spent her youth giving spiritualistic exhibitions while traveling with her parents' medicine and fortune-telling show. She married at fifteen, bore two children, divorced, married again, and then, in 1868, moved with her sister to New York City. In 1870 Victoria and her sister began the *Woodhull and Claflin's Weekly*, a newspaper that advocated equal rights for women, eight-hour workdays, graduated income tax, social welfare programs, and profit sharing. Victoria was full of contradictions. Though she owned the newspaper that first printed *The Communist Manifesto* in English, she was also the first female stockbroker on Wall Street.

In 1872, Victoria was nominated for the U.S. presidency by the Equal Rights party. Her candidacy attracted laborers, female suffragists, spiritualists, and communists. They were a diverse bunch who didn't agree on much other than wanting a government "of the people, by the people, and for the people."

Unfortunately, Victoria spent Election Day in jail. The U.S. government arrested her under the Comstock Act for sending "obscene" literature through the mail. The "obscenity" wasn't pornography, but rather an article about the renowned Reverend Henry Ward Beecher's affair with Lib Tilton, the wife of Beecher's best friend, Theodore Tilton. Ultimately, Victoria got tired of doing battle. She married for a third time and moved to England, where she started another magazine, *The Humanitarian*, with her daughter Zula.

I don't know what Victoria Woodhull would make of us today or what Sadie the Goat would have to say about the bunch of us collected here in these pages. And my mother sometimes shakes her head at what I do. But without these ladies, I'm not sure where we'd be.

Though we live in a world where honor killings (the practice of murdering one's sister, daughter, or wife if her "honor" has been sullied by, for example, rape) still goes on, the number of female warriors—pacifist and non—is growing. These women rush, head and heart first, through the barbed wire of age-old constrictions. And emerge battle scarred but luminous. This book is a celebration of that.

—Maggie Estep

Foreword

At times I wonder if I have any courage at all. The most dangerous thing I do is fly commercial. But the truth is that the world requires small acts of courage daily, so one cannot get too down about how big or small our acts of bravery are.

Still, I love to read stories of heroic feats. I am always excited to discover women who have sailed solo in the Vendée Globe race or made it to the peak of Mount Everest. And I like to read biographies of great, powerful women. They humble me but give me strength, too. I need to read about women who lived bravely and in doing so forged a trail that lead to the polling booth, to careers outside the home, to universities, to a seat in the senate, or in the cockpit, or, hell yes, at the bar. I now tread the path they carved with relative ease.

The first two volumes of Blanche Wisen Cooke's biography of Eleanor Roosevelt are kept in an old pie chest in my room. (Now, I've baked a pie or two in my time. In fact, I've baked exactly two. Everyone loves it when a woman bakes a pie. The trouble started when we asked for a piece of it.) I open those books occasionally and reread what Eleanor and her friends accomplished, how they led their lives, and I try to let the huge, powerful impact they had on the twentieth century and on my life today sink in. I hang on to Eleanor and the others like I would my seat cushion in the event of a water landing.

In my pie chest there are also books by Zora Neale Hurston, books about Josephine Baker and Dian Fossey and Mae West, all of whom are just a miniscule fraction of the women responsible for the path I follow today. I keep other books there, too. Poetry by Robert Frost and Anne Sexton, a biography of Miles Davis, Steinbeck's *The Grapes of Wrath*. I like to see them all together, on an equal foundation. I like to imagine the original owner of my pie cabinet, most likely a woman, and wonder about her work, too.

I have other feminine artifacts in my room: a pair of wooden Indian dolls, a tall, thoughtful female figure my sister sent me from Germany, and a pair of lotus slippers from the early 1900s I bought in San Francisco. The tiny shoes are a tragically small, sad bit of history, but I don't want to forget those women whose feet were bound in early childhood. They were barely able to walk and never danced or sailed or climbed. They claim this trail, too. So, to the girls and women who continue to forge on through this century, a reminder, if you will: Remember, please, and listen to the footsteps that led us here.

—Nora Dunn

Introduction

I'll start by telling you something about Phoolan Devi, the original Bandit Queen.

Phoolan Devi was born in 1957 into one of the lowest castes in India, a country that still adheres to a caste (class) system. Women born into such conditions have severely limited options. They are not taught to write or read, they will likely never travel away from home, and they are considered a burden for having not been born male. From the start, Phoolan exhibited behavior that made it clear she would not fit into this predetermined mold in a village so small (a few shacks built on the mud) that it isn't included on any maps of the area.

Disgusted by her father's refusal to fight for his family's land, which had been stolen from him by his own cousin, Phoolan became a rebel early on, warring with that cousin in an attempt to get the family land back. Presumably to get her out of the way, the same cousin convinced Phoolan's father to trade her as a bride at age eleven to a man three times her age in exchange for one cow. This man, her husband, beat and raped eleven-year-old Phoolan until, terrified and fed up, she ran back to her family. Disgraced by their daughter's actions (in traditional India a woman doesn't leave her husband), her parents suggested she commit suicide to restore the family honor. Refusing, Phoolan was marked as a renegade woman. In her teens she was incarcerated for a petty theft, and was brutalized and repeatedly raped by prison guards.

In 1979, Phoolan joined a gang of *dacoits*, or "armed bandits." It's debated whether she ran away or was kidnapped, but she eventually became the gang's leader. One of only three female *dacoit* leaders in India's history, she remains its most notorious. After a long career as outlaws, during which they allegedly committed theft and murder, Phoolan and her gang surrendered to the Indian government under very specific conditions. Breaching the terms of their agreement, the Indian government kept Phoolan imprisoned for the next eleven years without ever formally charging her with, or convicting her of, any crime.

After her release from prison, Phoolan reinvented herself as a politician at a time when the lower castes of India were desperate for better political representation. Phoolan's "Robin Hood" reputation (as a girl from desperately poor beginnings who rose to lead a band of rebel men against the upper castes) made her an ideal, albeit controversial, candidate, and in 1996 she won a seat in India's parliament.

To her detractors, Phoolan is a cruel, manipulative outlaw, one of the most dangerous women who ever lived. To her supporters, her legend is more important than the details of her criminal career. Women sing songs about the low-caste village girl who became a *dacoit* and was vindicated. She represents a determined unwillingness to accept the oppression fostered by the norms of society, and *that's* the spirit of what I'm trying to capture in this book.

This is a celebration of original thought and of the bravery it takes to live accordingly.

The unexamined life is not worth living. —Socrates

About two years ago I got really frustrated with my life. I was starting to make an impact as a musician, releasing albums and touring all over the world. And freelance photography was beginning to be a career instead of just a gaping hole into which I constantly poured money. However, like most people when they reach thirty, I took stock of my life and wondered whether I'd reach any of the goals I'd had for myself. The thing I found most lacking was a like-minded community with which to make art and personally grow.

I've always had (and still do have) a great group of smart, creative, talented friends, but somewhere along the way I had become surrounded by other people whose life philosophies just didn't jibe with mine. In my world as a musician, the girls who were friendly to me backstage were only talking to me to get to the boys in my band. The boys who were talking to me just wanted to do drugs (I never did) and to get to the boys in my band so they could promote their own bands.

As a photographer I would sometimes shoot tests for modeling agencies. I heard an alarming number of horror stories from very young models about how they'd been tormented by male photographers, made ashamed of their bodies, sometimes attacked, humiliated, and otherwise taken advantage of. I started to feel hypocritical and guilty for taking part in a system that would allow that to happen. I felt crazy, as if I was one of a very few who didn't like the way the world was set up. I needed desperately to inject myself into a group of people who might understand my frustrations and by whom I would feel inspired. I feared discovering that in order to "make it" in this world you had to think in accordance with all these values that I didn't believe in, specifically regarding sexism and exploitation. I needed to put the importance of my belief system over my need for any external affirmation. I wanted to celebrate people who live according to personal codes that I could relate to and respect, and who have each done at least one concrete thing that I feel gives women a stronger, smarter presence in a world often inclined to undervalue them. And that's what I'm doing with this book.

During my teenage years, a series of events conspired to shape my view of myself in destructive ways that are only now beginning to loosen their grip on me. Unfortunately, as I would later find is not uncommon, I was introduced to the complex world of sex and of myself as a sexual being through a mean and cold encounter with a boy to whom I couldn't have meant less. In response to the humiliation and frustration of my inability to change what had happened, I outwardly became a very tough, guarded girl. I shaved my head, got myself a tough, punk-rock boyfriend, and moved out to live with him at the age of sixteen, ending up in a three-year-long violent and dangerous relationship. In spite of the poor ways I was allowing myself to be treated, I always knew how I really felt everyone ought to be treated. Whether you're talking about relations between the sexes, races, or social classes, I've always been vocal and certain about my feelings and my expectations for equal treatment. The fact that there are still standards in place, perpetuated by unexamined traditions in thought, that allow so many women to be brutalized, disrespected, and otherwise used and abused is infuriating to me. I marvel at the inability of people involved in their own freedom struggles to extend those feelings related to their own victimization to the plights of others, specifically women.

Now I simply want to design my life so that I can live in accordance and peace with my truest beliefs. This book has gone a long way in helping me to reach that goal.

When I embarked on this project, my aim was to make an intensely personal and sincere piece of art. So it made sense to start with people I was most familiar with and to work outward from there, in the process expanding my own horizons. The first five women I approached, armed only with a concept, are all women who've been hugely influential in, and are iconic in, my art and music scene: Janeane Garofalo, Ann Magnuson, Maggie Estep, Exene Cervenka, and Lydia Lunch. Through various means, I contacted these women and told them I wanted to do a project about strong, smart women with varied approaches to living life as whole, complete people. Each woman responded with so much encouragement and generosity that what was initially intended to be a magazine article about great women soon evolved into a book that would tell a more complete story of my journey searching for role models and inspiration.

Doing this book has been an amazing adventure. It's enabled me to meet some of the incredible women whose work and way of thinking I admire. I got to speak with Donna Ferrato, one of my favorite photographers, about why we take pictures and what we think it means to photograph. I talked with Alice Walker about the parent/child relationship from both sides of the equation. I got into the boxing ring with Freeda George Foreman and got a taste of what it would actually feel like to be on the receiving end of her punches. I sat on the living-room floor of playwright Paula Vogel's home, played with her new puppy, and got to tell her exactly why her play How I Learned to Drive had affected me so profoundly. I laughed myself sick for an afternoon hanging out with Sandra Bernhard. I spent a morning with Sister Elaine Roulet in the mental ward of a women's prison asking the inmates and guards questions about prison life.

Photographing people gives you license to explore their lives in ways that you wouldn't be invited to do otherwise. When people let down their guard and allow me to photograph them, I feel honored. Having a picture of the time you spent with someone is an attempt to recapture what you shared and why it moved you. I hope the pictures included in this book have captured the essence of the time I spent with these remarkable women, what it meant to me, and why I think they're women whose work you may want to investigate further.

I asked each of these women, who have taken their own paths, to give us some insight into their guiding principles by writing something that could loosely be called a "law" or philosophy by which they try to live. The result is a unique look into the inner workings of a handful of the inspirational, original thinkers of our time. These women are Bandit Queens. Their laws are the framework for living life on their own terms, and not letting anyone else's ideas define them or hold them down.

My original Bandit Queen, Phoolan Devi, was driven, it seems, into a life of revenge and violence. But if something positive can be gleaned from her personal rebellion, it is her unwillingness to allow her spirit to be beaten down and defeated. I'm so glad that my eight-year-old stepdaughter and her friends run around with shirts that say GIRLS ROCK and GIRL POWER, and that they're proud and see their choices (I hope) as infinite. But the fact that "girl power" has swept over us as a media trend suggests that someday it will go the way of the pet rock or the hula hoop rather than be taken seriously as simply a natural evolution in thought for the advancement of humankind.

So here I am, writing this book to try to make a difference for the better, to show my appreciation to other people who have, and to inspire, because we all have the potential to be Bandit Queens.

Laws of the Bandit Queens

Aimee Mullins

Today I spent the day with Aimee Mullins in her tiny but cozy New York City apartment. At only twenty-five years old, Aimee is already a world-record holder in the 100- and 200-meter dashes and the long jump. She's spoken at the White House for National Girls and Women in Sports Day, was named one of the Top 100 Irish Americans of 1999 by *Irish America* magazine, and cofounded HOPE (Helping Others Perform with Excellence), a nonprofit organization that sponsors applicants with a variety of disabilities and whose mission statement is "to provide the means, training, and opportunity for persons with disabilities to compete in sports." She's been featured on numerous prestigious television shows and in magazines and has walked the runway for designer Alexander McQueen.

Aimee is also perhaps the world's best-known disabled athlete. A double amputee, Aimee was born without fibulae. Doctors said she would never be able to walk, and in the hope that prosthetics would give their daughter a better chance at mobility, Aimee's parents made the decision to have both her legs amputated below the knees when she was a baby. In addition to her flourishing athletic career, she is currently sought after as a model and says she hopes "to present the fashion and advertising worlds with an opportunity for diversity; to showcase feminine beauty in another form."

AIMEE
MULLINS'S
LAW:
EVERYTHING
IS SWEETER
WITH RISK.

Aimee has never been deterred from pursuing her dreams. Even in grade school she wore wooden prosthetics that enabled her to play softball, basketball, and football. When she got to Georgetown University, she had a set of metal sprinting legs designed for her that were modeled after the hind legs of a cheetah. Today I saw those legs, as well as a set of her cosmetic legs, which appear alarmingly real and make her look like any number of other beautiful, blond, incredibly fit women walking around New York City. There is nothing obvious that sets her apart, except for the depth she exhibits, which is rare in such a young woman. Aimee says she thinks it's every person's duty to investigate and improve herself. She's paraphrasing Ghandi when she tells me that "you must be the change you wish to see in the world. So many people bitch and moan about things, but they never stick their necks out to change them."

Alice Walker

"It is painful to realize [that my parents and grand-
parents] were forever trying to correct a 'flaw' — that
of being black, female, human—that did not exist, except
as men of greed, misogyny, and violence defined it.
In my work I create characters who . . . explore what
it would feel like not to be imprisoned by the hatred
of women, the love of violence, the destructiveness
of greed." —from *Anything We Love Can Be Saved*

ALICE WALKER'S LAWS:
1. DEATH IS THE DIREC-
TION WE ARE ALWAYS
FACING. BECAUSE OF
THIS I STROLL LEISURELY.
2. THE RIGHT TO EXIST
AS I AM IS FUNDAMEN-
TAL. MY PRESENCE
PROVES IT. 3. I AM CER-
TAIN THAT WE WERE
MEANT TO BE CREATIVE,
TO MAKE LOVE, TO SING
AND DANCE AND PLAY.
EVERYTHING ELSE WAS
DREAMED UP FOR US.

Alice Walker has long written eloquently about women who have suffered physical, emotional, and sexual abuse, the kind that rips apart their sense of self, and that must be overcome if they are to reconnect body and soul. Her stories are microcosms in which larger sociopolitical issues are played out and gracefully condemned. "I love and adore the masculine as I love and adore the feminine," she tells me. "The masculine I love and adore is playful. The feminine I love and adore loves to play. I do not believe in, support, or condone male planetary leadership. I will never believe in a political social system that does not believe in me."

Alice's beautiful, piercing eyes, one brown, the other an unusual shade of gray, fix intensely on mine as she talks. She is spilling out what seem like pearls, which I'm lucky enough to hear and which I should be committing to memory. Yet she adamantly asserts that she has as much to learn from others as people have to learn from her. "I view each new friendship and especially each new lover as an opportunity to be completely reeducated," she tells me. I've been enriched by my one meeting with her. She spends more time listening than she does talking, and her constant appreciation for everything she sees around her makes me more appreciative of it as well. We talk as I take her picture. She's amazed by the ornate beauty of the rooftops on the midtown buildings that surround us that goes unnoticed by so many busy New Yorkers getting to work, and she keeps stopping in mid-conversation to point out her favorite details in them as we shoot.

When I first contacted her about being involved in this book she said, "Anything that calls me a Bandit Queen, I want to be a part of."

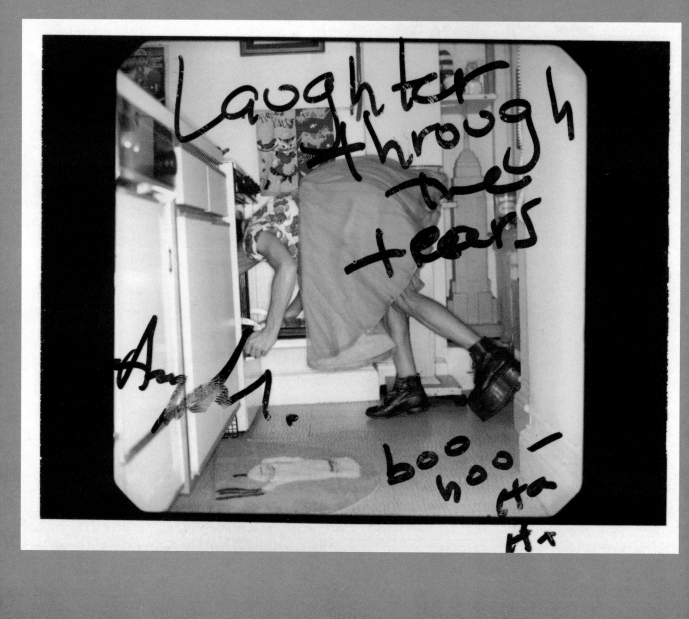

Amy Sedaris

If you're not already a fan of Amy Sedaris, it may be hard to understand why people are sold on her genius when she's best known as Jerri Blank, the offensive forty-four-year-old high-school student on the hit cable show *Strangers with Candy*. Jerri Blank is a loser who is the only one who doesn't perceive herself as such. In fact she quite likes herself, and we like her because she believes the voices that are ringing in her own head telling her she's okay over anything she hears from the outside world.

AMY SEDARIS'S LAW:
LAUGHTER THROUGH THE TEARS.

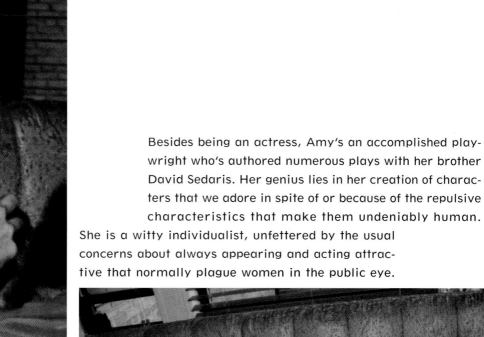

Besides being an actress, Amy's an accomplished playwright who's authored numerous plays with her brother
David Sedaris. Her genius lies in her creation of characters that we adore in spite of or because of the repulsive
characteristics that make them undeniably human.
She is a witty individualist, unfettered by the usual
concerns about always appearing and acting attrac-
tive that normally plague women in the public eye.

It was fascinating to watch her transform herself from a polite, pretty, petite, Southern girl who was a Girl Scout until the age of fourteen into a dozen-odd characters for our photos. Out came the nicotine tooth stain and the fake braces and the matted wigs and the orthopedic shoes, one sole one inch high, the other one six inches high (she paused to reflect on how sad it was that someone had actually had to wear them). It was like playing dress up with your friend at five years old. Except it's the friend your mom isn't crazy about because even though she knows she's a nice girl, she senses that maybe she's a little bit troubled, considering the way she sometimes talks to herself and seems to hear someone answering.

Ann Magnuson

Ann Magnuson is both a
product of pop culture and
a critic of it. She mocks it in
her bizarre cabaret extrav-
aganzas, which combine
song, dance, storytelling
(always with an incisive
wit), and usually something
to do with outer space.

To take Ann's portrait, I constructed what I saw as the ideal Ann Magnuson set—contrived, theatrical, and a bit decadent. She arrived, took one look at it, and asked if we could destroy it for the pictures. As I stood there, mouth agape, artist's ego bruised, she pointed out that while this set did successfully capture the image she'd created for herself in the 1980s, one that lovingly satirized popular cultural iconography, she said she wasn't really at that point either personally or professionally anymore. So we ransacked the set and it became the Electric Blue Lobster, a nightclub in hell at which Ann was working the door.

The character in the shot is a woman who's seen a little too much, stayed out a little too late for a little too long. Still she emerges glamorous and victorious, a little banged up and tired, but a lot wiser, too.

ANN MAGNUSON'S LAW:
DO IT ALL AND LET GOD

SORT IT OUT!

Bust Magazine Founders

I first picked up *Bust* magazine because Janeane Garofalo was on the cover and her image seemed incongruous with the title. I was immediately drawn in. *Bust* turned out to be accessible to a wide audience while remaining true to its purpose of providing education and entertainment for people who care about what it's like to be a girl. The articles on practical sex tips, relationships, career, and women and men we love are well written and down-to-earth. The magazine's focus is young women, but it isn't so narrow as to exclude others. It educates rather than simply preaches to the converted.

Bust was founded in 1993 by Laurie Henzel, Marcelle Karp, and Debbie Stoller.

Marcelle explains, "I don't know if there will ever be true equality and harmony among women and men in my lifetime. I don't know if I will ever see a world without rape and abuse and everything that goes along with that. But I have no intention of giving up. Because no matter what label I assign myself—mother, daughter, sister, wife, friend, teacher, student—I will always be a woman, and that lays the groundwork for everything else."

BUST MAGAZINE'S LAW: WOMEN NEED TO BREAK DOWN AS MANY STIGMAS ABOUT FEMINISM AS POSSIBLE AND TO EMBRACE ALL THE POSSIBILITIES AND OPPORTUNITES WE HAVE.

Carol Kaye

Carol Kaye was a highly respected member of the group of L.A. session musicians known as the "clique," (more commonly called The Wrecking Crew, a name coined by drummer Hal Blaine). These "first call" musicians played on many of the numerous pop hits to come out of L.A. in the 1960s. If there's a bass line you've ever noticed and remembered, chances are good that Carol played it

In 1963, after having already established herself as a successful L.A. jazz guitarist with five years of studio guitar work, Carol picked up the electric bass when someone didn't show up at a Capitol Records session. The electric bass was relatively new to the studio, and Carol says she imagined parts for it that no one else was playing. It was then that she started playing the inventive bass lines she's become known for. Carol is credited with more than ten thousand recording sessions in all, having played on numerous quintessential recordings with the Beach Boys, Phil Spector, Elvis Presley, the Monkees, Nancy Sinatra, Sonny and Cher, Quincy Jones, Joe Cocker, Herb Alpert, and the Supremes, and on several hundred recognizable theme songs for movies and television programs like *Mission Impossible, M*A*S*H, Hawaii 5-0,* and the original *Thomas Crown Affair.*

The music world has always been ahead of its time in breaking down barriers. Musicians tend to respect one another's talents irrespective of race or gender. Carol has known a lot of fine female jazz musicians and they were always well respected. "Whether or not you could play was the bottom line."

But women did face some obstacles that men didn't. For instance, in the late 1950s and early 1960s "a woman wasn't anything if she didn't get married," she says. "So a lot of the girls played until they got married and then that was it. Once the Pill came along, that changed a lot because women had more choices." Carol's been married three times and has never quit playing. Though she had to sell her first Gibson Super 400 bass to pay the hospital bills when she had her baby, by the 1960s she was making an impressive $75,000 annually, more than most of her male peers. "In the studio, if the men started giving you a hard time, you'd just give it right back to them good."

CAROL KAYE'S LAW: LIVE YOUR
LIFE IN TRUTH AND TAKE CARE
OF YOUR RESPONSIBILITIES
FIRST. THINGS ALWAYS WORK
OUT. DON'T DRINK OR SMOKE
OR USE DRUGS. BE GOOD TO
OTHER PEOPLE. TRY TO BE
TOLERANT—YOU DON'T KNOW
WHAT OTHER PEOPLE HAVE
BEEN THROUGH. BE A GOOD
PROFESSIONAL WITH LOTS OF
HUMOR. DON'T LET SOMEONE
DERIDE YOU WITHOUT FEEDING
IT BACK TO THEM. AND
ALWAYS PLAY YOUR TAIL
OFF—THE MONEY WILL COME.

Cheryl Haworth

Bob Haworth is beaming with pride as he talks about his three talented daughters, all accomplished athletes, artists, and musicians well before the age of twenty. On track to becoming the strongest woman in the world is Cheryl Haworth, who holds every U.S. weight-lifting record in her weight class and who brought home the bronze medal for weight lifting at the 2000 Summer Olympics, the first time the competition was opened to women. "Olympic glory," Cheryl says, "shouldn't be all men's. I don't think there should be any gender issues in sports."

When Cheryl was twelve, her dad took her to the gym so she could get in shape for the upcoming softball season. The Team Savannah women's weight lifters were working out there and the idea of weight lifting immediately appealed to Cheryl. It was a perfect match, and neither of her parents had any misgivings about her taking it up.

At seventeen (an age rife with issues about body image), standing five-foot-nine and weighing 295 pounds, Cheryl is an extremely well-adjusted, calm, and confident young woman. It's a great sign of the times that she's become a role model for members of the Girl Scouts, an organization founded and intrinsically tied up in the history of Cheryl's hometown of Savannah, Georgia. Her attitude and accomplishments help to pave the way for young girls to view their potential and opportunities as limitless.

We shot these pictures at the home of Juliette Gordon Low, the founder of the Girl Scouts. It was Cheryl, me, three Girl Scouts, and about twenty-five parents, onlookers, and members of the media. Everyone was interested in Cheryl.

CHERYL HAWORTH'S LAW: IF YOU ARE BEING DISCOURAGED, YOU SHOULDN'T WORRY ABOUT IT. I KNOW A LOT OF PEOPLE JUST AUTOMATICALLY ASSUMED THAT BECAUSE I WAS SO BIG, FOR ME TO EXCEL IN ANYTHING PHYSICAL, ESPECIALLY A SPORT, WOULD BE ALMOST IMPOSSIBLE. BUT I JUST FOUND SOMETHING I WAS GOOD AT AND DIDN'T LET ANYTHING STOP ME.

Donna Ferrato

For me, Donna Ferrato's *Living with the Enemy* is one
of the most important, most successful photo essays
in the history of photography. Donna's latest project,
called *Love and Lust* (her two favorite subjects, she
says), is a departure from the documenting of domestic violence that's largely defined her career so far.
My favorite photo in *Living with the Enemy* is of a couple
Donna was staying with, caught in the act of a violent fight
in their completely mirrored bathroom. Alerted by the
screams of the woman, Donna rushed in and took the picture
just as the man smacked the woman hard across the face,
undaunted by the fact that someone was photographing them.

DONNA FERRATO'S LAW: I LIVE LIKE AN
OF LOVE, FOR PASSION WITHOUT
THIS ROAD IS THE ONLY

OUTLAW FOR THE EMANCIPATION
OPPRESSION.
ONE I EVER WISH TO KNOW.

Many people wonder how documentary photographers and filmmakers can stand by and record horror and violence without stopping to help the victims, and yet in Donna's case it could be argued that the impact of that single image, and its potential to effect change, has done more for the plight of domestically abused women than anything she could have done in that situation. (In a previous interview Donna made it clear that after getting that amazing shot, in which she is also visible in the reflection of the bathroom mirror, she put down her camera to help. She was violently thrown to the ground for her efforts.)

I loved meeting her. She was sensitive, encouraging, open, and up for anything so that I could get an interesting shot of her.

ESG

The Scroggins sisters grew up in the projects of the South Bronx in the 1970s. Surrounded as they were by gang violence and poverty, what could have been a narrow view of the world was broadened, first, by watching Don Kirshner's *Rock Concert* religiously, and second, by a mother whose determination to keep her daughters out of trouble prompted her to buy them a set of instruments, which they then taught themselves to play. Practice took place daily in their small apartment, and before long the band ESG was born. (The birthstones of the sisters are emerald, sapphire, and amethyst. Renee says they changed "amethyst" to "gold" because they wanted to make gold records, and used the three initials as the name of the band.) Though at first they played mostly covers, Renee Scroggins says that they eventually stopped doing this since "if people recognized the song you were trying to play, they could tell when you were doing it badly. If it was your own, they would just think you'd come up with some crazy new kind of experimental music."

After a while, the noise started to sound pretty good and the Scrogginses' matriarch had to shoo the gathering crowds away from the apartment door when they'd gather to listen.

Since the oldest among the sisters was only nineteen when they started playing in New York City underground clubs like Danceteria and the Peppermint Lounge, their mom not only had to drive them to their gigs, but she had to chaperone, keeping them backstage and out of the clubs in which they weren't allowed to be. During these years they played with bands like the Gang of Four, the Bush Tetras, the Clash, and Public Image Limited. It was a time when the delineations between types of music were blurred and it seemed everyone was trying a little of everything: punk, disco, reggae, blues. . . . The experimental, totally original sound of ESG embraces this openness and willingness to merge forms, conceptually and musically.

RENEE SCROGGINS'S LAW: YOU ARE THE RULER OF YOUR OWN DESTINY. IF YOU WANT SOMETHING IN LIFE, YOU HAVE TO GO OUT AND GET IT, BECAUSE IT'S JUST NOT GOING TO COME OVER AND KISS YOU ON YOUR LIPS.

MARIE SCROGGINS'S LAW:
EDUCATE YOURSELF

BECAUSE IGNORANCE IS SLAVERY.

Two of the original members have now been replaced by Renee's and Valerie's teenage daughters, making the full lineup Renee, her sisters Marie and Valerie, Renee's daughter Nicole, and Valerie's daughter Chistelle.

"We got an offer to open up for Public Image Limited when Valerie [the drummer] was in her ninth month," Renee tells me. "I told the guy I wasn't sure, I'd have to ask her, but I kind of doubted she could do it. She asked me how much they were gonna pay, and when I told her she said, 'Yeah, I can make it!' So we played and it made for some really interesting arrangements. We'd be into a song and all of a sudden the baby would kick and it'd make Valerie hang on a beat a little too long or something, and I'd turn around and say 'Alright! That was really cool.' And we'd keep it in the song."

Exene Cervenka

Exene Cervenka influenced almost every woman I know in her formative years, and continues, both with the records she made with her seminal band, X, and on her own, to have an impact on new audiences. She's been a punk, a poet, a wife, a mother. She virtually invented the look of the American punk woman. She's mysterious, original, and smart. Her songs show compassion for and association with the working class and people forgotten by an often cruel and greedy world. She sings most often on behalf of those struggling to survive and grabbing bits of beauty for themselves in the form of love and affection where they can find it.

Exene merged the dramatic look of a 1920s film star with that of 1970s punk rocker, and millions of us eagerly followed suit, identifying with her rather than with other female icons of the time, such as Madonna. She and her then-husband, John Doe, were our punk-rock Romeo and Juliet. Exene never downplayed her intelligence, talent, or opinions. The many who eagerly identified with her questioned to what degree their beauty and worth should be measured by their overt sexuality. Rather than being appendages to artistic boyfriends, they regarded themselves as the artists, the thinkers, the justifiably disgruntled people. For some reason I was kind of surprised by how incredibly funny Exene is. I had a couple of adventures with her after we met doing this photo shoot and she definitely has an Exene universe going on in her head that takes in information, interprets it in her own, unique way, and spits it back out at you, more interesting than when it went in.

EXENE CERVENKA'S LAW:
IF I EVER DID MANAGE TO FIND A LAW TO LIVE BY, I WOULD BREAK IT.

Freeda George Foreman

Freeda George Foreman (named after her father, boxer George Foreman, like most of her eight brothers and sisters) met me at the gym in Denver where she trains, her five-year-old daughter Justice in tow. She looked stunning when she showed up, hardly like the tough brawler I'd expected. After disappearing into the locker room, one she shares with the many men she works out alongside of, she reemerged still looking quite beautiful, but also alarmingly like her father. They share the same powerful, solid arms that deliver powerful, solid punches in the ring, and both have a similar calm, confident look in their eyes.

Initially dismayed by his daughter's decision to box, George Foreman tried to dissuade her by offering her a check that matched the winning purse of her first bout with the condition that she back out of the fight. It wasn't about the money for her, so she continued fighting, and over time, as her father observed her enthusiasm and talent, he became much more supportive. As Freeda trained and I photographed, her daughter worked out tirelessly on the heavy bag next to her, saying things to the bag like "You want a piece of me?" She wants to be a boxer, too, and has no reason to think she couldn't grow up to be one.

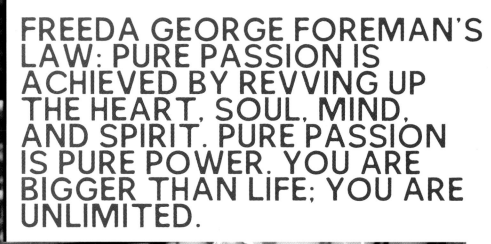

FREEDA GEORGE FOREMAN'S LAW: PURE PASSION IS ACHIEVED BY REVVING UP THE HEART, SOUL, MIND, AND SPIRIT. PURE PASSION IS PURE POWER. YOU ARE BIGGER THAN LIFE; YOU ARE UNLIMITED.

Geraldine Ferraro

The first thing that struck me about Geraldine Ferraro when we met was how physically small she is. I guess I'd imagined that the woman who, in 1984, made history as the first woman ever to run for the office of vice president of the United States on a major political party's ticket would be more imposing.

What she did reveal herself to be was self-confident, well informed, friendly in a straight-forward, New York kind of way, and busy—very busy. Within ten minutes she was gone. The second she left, my assistant, who was born in France, blurted out a million questions she thought I should have asked her. Did Ms. Ferraro think the United States was ready for a female president? Why was the United States so far behind so many other countries, which at some point or another had had female figureheads? What did she think about the Bush versus Gore debacle the country was currently embroiled in? I immediately felt like a dunce, that I had wasted a valuable opportunity to pick the brain of this historical figure. Instead I had talked with her about family, photography, and life in general in New York. But that, too, had its value—I got to see another side of her that created a more complete picture. This picture of her as an average woman with normal concerns impressed upon me just how attainable goals like running for vice president are.

In addition to her vice presidential campaign, Ms. Ferraro also started the Special Victims Bureau in the Queens County District Attorney's Office, which specializes in prosecuting sex crimes, child abuse, domestic abuse, and crimes against the elderly, and as a three-term congresswoman, she spearheaded efforts to have the ERA passed and sponsored the Women's Economic Equity Act.

In 2001, Geraldine Ferraro revealed publicly that she's been battling an incurable form of cancer called multiple myeloma since 1998. A bone cancer that usually results in the death of its sufferers within only a few years of its diagnosis, the cancer is currently in remission and kept somewhat at bay because it was diagnosed and she was able to start treatment early. She exhibited her trademark strength of character in a recent interview, saying "This is a race I may not win, but I've lost other races before, so it's not the end of the world." She also said she hopes to survive long enough "to attend the inauguration of the first woman president of the United States."

GERALDINE FERRARO'S LAW: MY MOM ALWAYS TOLD ME: SET YOUR GOALS HIGH. AND IF, FOR SOME REASON, YOU DON'T GET WHAT YOU WANT, DON'T LOOK BACK— MOVE ON.

The Guerilla Girls

When I first saw the (original) *Planet of the Apes*, I was completely terrified by those gorilla warriors charging on horseback. It was and still is
one of the scariest images I've ever seen. The day I was to meet "Frida
Khalo" of the Guerrilla Girls in front of the Guggenheim Museum in New
York City, she was casually walking down the street to meet me wearing
a ferocious, screaming gorilla mask, and I experienced a strong sense-
memory panic reaction. "We joined a long tradition of masked avengers,"
Frida tells me. "No one knows who we are or where we will strike next."
The Guerilla Girls attack racist and sexist curating practices, socially
sanctioned sexism, and censorship through humorous yet provacative
advertising and poster campaigns. The group was formed in 1985 in
response to the Museum of Modern Art's "An International Survey of Painting and Sculpture," a show meant to be an up-to-the-minute summary of
the most significant contemporary art in the world, but one in which almost
all the artists were white, either from Europe or the United States, and
only thirteen of the 169 included were women. The Guerrilla Girls argue
that because the art world reflects and comments on the culture around it,
a male-centric and racist culture is reflected in the standards used to judge
art. "We think the art that's in museums and galleries should tell the whole
story of our culture and not just the white male part," "Frida" says.

The members of the notorious Guerrilla Girls take their pseudonyms from deceased
female artists and writers such as Frida Kahlo, Alice Neel, and Zora Neale Hurston,
thus keeping their true identities hidden. Anonymity gives them carte blanche to
publicly attack the curating policies of the art world's biggest institutions, and their
pseudonyms keep alive the memory of these sometimes forgotten women.

One of their most widely recognized posters reads DO WOMEN HAVE TO BE NAKED TO
GET INTO THE METROPOLITAN MUSEUM? and shows a gorilla mask placed on a
famous 19th-century painting of an odalisque by Ingres. Their most recent book,
The Guerrilla Girls' Bedside Companion to the History of Western Art, takes a look
at two thousand years of art history, addresses such subjects as the ways in which
social obstacles and sexist historians have impeded the progress of women artists,
and celebrates the courageous individuals who've succeeded in spite of them.

As I talked with "Frida Kahlo," I searched for a comfortable, inviting place
on the gorilla mask to focus on. I couldn't find one and so resorted to trying not to look panicked. A woman in her thirties slowed down as she passed
and eventually, sheepishly asked, "Are you a real Guerrilla Girl?" When the
answer was yes, she was elated and gushing with gratitude for all the good
that the group has done on behalf of women artists. She left beaming.

THE GUERRILLA GIRLS' LAW: ANY VETERAN OF THE CIVIL RIGHTS, WOMEN'S, OR GAY RIGHTS MOVEMENTS KNOWS THAT PROGRESS IS THE RESULT OF PRESSURE, PROTEST, AND STRUGGLE. **PERSEVERE.**

Jane Pratt

With recurring columns entitled "Makeunders" and "Do-it-Yourself-Fashion," *Jane* magazine stands out as decidedly more irreverent and humane than other magazines when it comes to issues of fashion and beauty. That difference in tone was more pronounced in 1997 when *Jane* started, but recently some of the more traditional magazines have begun to imitate *Jane*'s unique voice.

Jane magazine is the brainchild of Jane Pratt, the majority of whose career has been intrinsically linked with exploring the lives of young girls and women. At twenty-four, Jane started *Sassy*, a magazine known for its intelligent and humorous approach to dealing with difficult issues that teenagers face. She's also authored two books on growing up female, *For Real: The Uncensored Truth about America's Teenagers*, and *Beyond Beauty: Girls Speak Out on Looks, Style, and Stereotypes*.

Jane is captain of an enormous ship whose crew is the production staff of *Jane* magazine, a division of Fairchild Publications. There are rows and rows of cubicles with people typing and talking and racing from place to place. Then out of the executive office comes this fun-looking girl. We immediately start chatting and gossiping and laughing, and it's easy to forget what an empire she's created.

Jane shared her thoughts on marriage with me: "I read somewhere recently that ninety-five percent of women are dying to get married, and I feel so lucky that my feminist mom raised me in that other five percent, so much without that marriage goal that I can't even grasp the concept that being married is somehow inherently better for a woman than not being married. And if we raise our daughters that way, I can only think they'll make smarter choices about who they marry or don't. And they'll be happier before, during, and/or after."

JANE PRATT'S LAW: ANOTHER WOMAN'S SUCCESS IS A SUCCESS FOR US ALL. BEING A WOMAN'S WOMAN ALL THE TIME MEANS NEVER COMPETING WITH ANOTHER WOMAN, 'CAUSE IF YOU'RE COMPETING FOR A JOB, YOU'RE HOLDING US ALL BACK. PLEASE MAKE ROOM FOR BOTH OF YOU. IF YOU'RE COMPETING FOR THE SAME MAN/WOMAN, WHAT THE WINNER'S GETTING IS NO PRIZE. IF YOU'RE COMPETING IN SOME DEEPER, VAGUER SENSE WITH, SAY, EVERY WOMAN OUT THERE—TO BE PRETTIER, GET MARRIED SOONER, OR LOOK YOUNGER LONGER—YOU ARE LIVING IN THE DARK AGES.

Janeane Garofalo

Years ago, I was watching some silly daytime talk show that had a panel of "experts."
Most of them were very well-known women, although I can't remember any of them
now. They were there to provide inane pabulum in response to the host's supposedly
riveting and provocative questions about women and what we think of various successful ones. When they reached the inevitable subject of Madonna (I think it was
around the time Madonna's *Sex* book had been released), all the women on the panel
stumbled over one another to brown their noses in the crack of Madonna's well-
publicized butt. "Oh, she's a genius." "If she were a man, they wouldn't call her a
bitch." "She's a visionary." When the as-yet-quiet, relatively unknown panelist on the
end farthest from the host piped up to say, "I don't think there's anything new about
using sex to sell yourself," the other women on the stage all looked as if she'd personally slapped each of them across the face. The host barely acknowledged the com-
ment, and after two beats continued on with the discussion as if the panelist had never
spoken. I, on the other hand, jumped to attention and wanted to know who she was.

JANEANE GAROFALO'S LAW: "NO ONE CAN MAKE YOU FEEL INFERIOR WITHOUT YOUR CONSENT." —ELEANOR ROOSEVELT SAID IT AND IT'S SOMETHING I TRY TO REMEMBER EVERY DAY.

Obviously, since that brief television appearance years ago, Janeane Garofalo has made her mark as a versatile actor, comedian, and social satirist, and people listen to what she has to say. She's attained an admirable type of celebrity, one in which she retains her individuality but still benefits from a good measure of recognizability and opportunity. She's able to be a mainstream artist while at the same time, in her stand-up, she criticizes the entertainment industry and what it does to women in particular.

In her stand-up act one time, Janeane commented on a fashion reviewer who'd outraged her by saying "A pretty face is your best asset on the runway this year!" You could just hear the anger making her voice tremble as she retorted, "Oh yeah! Last year ugly girls really got a *free ride!*"

I am forever grateful to her for being the first person to say yes to being involved in this project. She had interviewed my band a few months earlier for a radio show she does and I managed to finagle a phone number from her publicist. When I called her about it she said, "Sure, as long as there's no hair, makeup, or stylist." (These are dream words to any ambitious yet struggling artist.)

"I'm trying," Janeane says, "to be one of the few people in my job who doesn't make teenage girls feel bad about themselves." Perhaps she's a reluctant hero, but Janeane Garofalo has definitely become a hero to many of us even so. She's always herself, always funny and unafraid to voice her opinion, even when it grates against the norms of the identity-warping, homogenizing entertainment industry. She is genuine and we root for her success.

Jocelyn Elders

Jocelyn Elders grew up in extraordinary poverty, one of eight children who started working at a very young age. Instead of being limited by this start, she was motivated to have a better life, aided by her mother's determination that all of her children receive a good education.

The only woman in a class of one hundred, and one of only three African-Americans, she attended the University of Arkansas Medical School on a scholarship. She has worked with Hillary Rodham Clinton on several women's advocacy programs, and on her own for sex education and access to better immunization and prenatal care. During the Clinton administration she was appointed the first female African-American Surgeon General, but when, in the hopes of reducing unplanned pregnancy and the spread of AIDS, she suggested that masturbation (in addition to abstinence) be taught in sex education classes, there was a huge public uproar. People apparently thought that her proposal called into question her morality, and President Clinton requested her resignation.

JOCELYN ELDERS' LAW: ALWAYS DO YOUR BEST. THAT'S GOOD ENOUGH.

The idea of working at the level that she has in government is so entirely outside of my realm of experience that I was extremely nervous and uncomfortable when I showed up for my meeting with her. It didn't help my nerves that while I was twenty minutes early, I was told she would be leaving for dinner in five minutes, so I'd better hurry up if I wanted to catch her. But then from the center of a team of harried, anxious, pushy handlers, one of whom alerted her to my arrival, Jocelyn Elders spun around and gave me a huge, warm smile and a wave. During our five minutes together she showed herself to be open, friendly, and very down-to-earth.

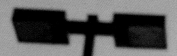

Karen Duffy

In the early 1990s Karen Duffy was known as "Duff," an irreverent, wisecracking, bawdy MTV VJ. She was also a Revlon spokesmodel and a news correspondent on Michael Moore's *TV Nation*, had acting roles in movies like *Dumb and Dumber* and *Reality Bites*, and had a sit-com and a project with Disney in development. She was extremely independent, enjoyed a hectic schedule, and was driven to succeed and to enjoy life to its fullest.

Then, in 1995, what started as a bad headache quickly progressed into extreme pain and eventually into a diagnosis of sarcoidosis, an incurable, life-threatening illness of the central nervous system. Karen says that before treatment began to alleviate some of her physical pain, the disease caused her skin to be so unbearably sensitive to touch that it felt as though she were "constantly boiling in oil."

Devastated at first by having to face her own mortality while only in her early thirties, she began to use her trademark dark, quirky sense of humor to keep her spirits up. Often she arrived at the hospital for treatment in formal wear, a tiara, and pearls, and she confused (and frightened) hospital workers by keeping a picture of Dr. Kevorkian (the "suicide doctor") over her hospital bed. Her life had been completely altered, but she did what she could to alleviate some of the fear and sadness that had descended upon her, her family, and her friends.

I don't want to reduce her life's achievements to how well she's dealt in the face of extreme adversity. Prior to her diagnosis, she'd proven herself an engaging, charismatic talent. But her consequential strength is inspirational and deserves celebration.

Three days after we shot, Karen had to go back into the hospital for another major operation, after which she'd start another round of chemotherapy, a treatment she'd endured numerous times: "You get used to it. It's like going to the dentist. Everyone's afraid to go to the dentist, but once you get there it's no big deal. You just do it."

During our shoot, she told me about the annual California road trip she takes with her best friend. They are ostensibly in search of Frank Sinatra's monogrammed golf shirts they hope may have been donated to thrift stores by his charitable widow, Barbara. Each of them spends five dollars a day at a thrift store to dress the other in whatever she likes. As a result, Karen was wearing a muumuu and cat's-eye glasses and her friend was dressed in a Hooters uniform with a trucker's hat that said WINE 'EM, DINE 'EM, SIXTY-NINE 'EM! when she decided to try to scam their way into the gift shop at the Betty Ford Clinic (she says she thought it would make for some great gifts). Charming her way past the guards, she ended up buying several hundred dollars' worth of BETTY FORD CLINIC jogging suits and, so as not to arouse suspicion, grabbed the first self-help book she saw, titled *Stinking Thinking*. Much to her surprise, she gleaned some wisdom from the book.

KAREN DUFFY'S LAW: *STINKING THINKING* IS WHERE I BECAME HIP TO THE IDEA THAT YOU BECOME WHAT YOU THINK ABOUT THE MOST. I THINK IT'S TRUE.

Kim Shattuck

In an unassuming corner of her kitchen, under a three-tier
hanging fruit basket, wedged in behind the refrigerator on
which she's hung a huge poster of Albert Einstein, is where
Kim Shattuck, lead singer, songwriter, and guitarist for the
aggressive pop band the Muffs, has written and recorded
demos for what her devotees would call her greatest hits.

She dresses like an enormous little kid and writes great pop songs
about revenge, confusion, and ex-boyfriends. Her ferocious,
direct delivery earns her constant comparisons to Joan Jett and
Courtney Love (although Kim is my favorite of the three).

"I love writing
songs and taking
photographs,"
Kim Shattuck
tells me. "I would
die if I couldn't."

A member of the Pandoras, a mid-eighties pop band, and founder of the Muffs in the early nineties, Kim's been dubbed an "Indie Queen Icon." But when asked in an interview about what it's like to be a female musician, she was quick to say, "It's a relief to be taken as a musician first, because when they think of you as a 'bimbo' or a 'sex kitten,' nobody listens." Kim cares about being heard, and she'll always tell you exactly what she thinks. When the boys in the crowd scream, "Show us your tits!" or try to look up her skirt, she kicks them in the head from the front of the stage. She's autonomous, never having been defined by a musical movement like Riot Girl, one that many of her contemporaries started or joined in response to the sexism and homophobia they saw in the music scene. When asked about the idea of her participating in Lilith Fair, she said, "I'm not going braless. I'm a D-cup."

Kim's reputation for being volatile and impulsive precedes her, but to me she was, although certainly a strong personality, nothing but nice, funny, and great.

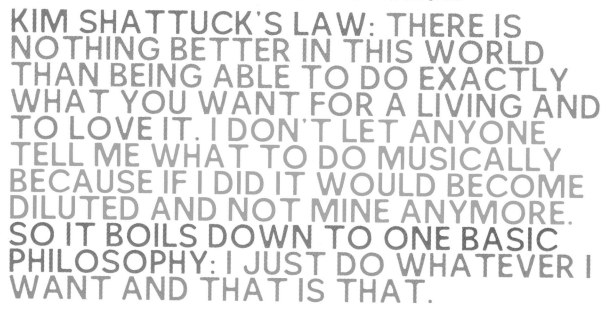

KIM SHATTUCK'S LAW: THERE IS NOTHING BETTER IN THIS WORLD THAN BEING ABLE TO DO EXACTLY WHAT YOU WANT FOR A LIVING AND TO LOVE IT. I DON'T LET ANYONE TELL ME WHAT TO DO MUSICALLY BECAUSE IF I DID IT WOULD BECOME DILUTED AND NOT MINE ANYMORE. SO IT BOILS DOWN TO ONE BASIC PHILOSOPHY: I JUST DO WHATEVER I WANT AND THAT IS THAT.

Linda Ellerbee

Linda Ellerbee has been an outspoken journalist for more than thirty years, known for her integrity and her sense of humor. She currently produces, writes, and hosts *Nick News,* which airs on Nickelodeon and is the longest-running children's news program in television history. Her production company, Lucky Duck, is the largest supplier of *Intimate Portraits* for the Lifetime channel and the largest supplier of *Headliners and Legends,* hosted by Matt Lauer on MSNBC. Recently she developed a twelve-part HBO series on the women's movement of the 1960s and '70s. She's published two best-selling books. The first, *And So It Goes,* looks at the world of TV news and is used as a textbook in more than a hundred colleges, and the second, *Move On,* chronicles her life as a single, working mother and a child of the sixties. She's also authored a series of books called Get Real about a middle-school girl who's a reporter for her school paper. Linda dreamed of being a reporter when she was young.

In 1982 Linda had a cancer scare and doctors performed a biopsy that turned out negative. She left the hospital relieved and saw a little toy duck in a gift shop window that she said she was sure smiled at her, so she ran right in and bought it. Unfortunately, ten years later she was diagnosed with breast cancer and underwent a double mastectomy. She has survived, physically and emotionally, and the duck continues to be passed around to every sick family member and friend. That is when it's not busy appearing somewhere in each episode of *Nick News*. It is what her company, Lucky Duck Productions, is named after. As a survivor, she's become an outspoken advocate for breast cancer research and has brought her humanity and humor to other women with cancer, talking with them at great length about surviving the experience.

In the author bio of one of the books in the Get Real series, Linda writes, "My mother . . . was totally hard to please; therefore, I wanted to please her. . . . We were different. . . . I kept on trying to be more of the girl she wanted, a girl who cared about dolls, dresses, tutus, tea parties, and hair curlers—not someone who cared about running with the wind, painting pictures, having adventures, boys. . . . I've nothing against a tutu. . . . And I don't really mind dresses . . . or dolls. . . . And of course I used hair curlers. . . . The thing was, I merely did not wish to be defined by these things, or confined to them."

I arrived in the midst of a very hectic day at Lucky Duck Productions. It was the day that the United States should have had a new president but only had a tie, and Linda was rushing to prepare a news program to inform kids about this history-making event. I'd come equipped with three Styrofoam heads as props, which I then had to stand around with for an hour, feeling intrusive and a little silly. To be honest, I'm not even sure why I had them except that I had a sense of how different she is from the usual news anchor "talking heads," and so somehow it made sense to me. When she was finally able to join me, with only ten minutes to allow for our shoot, she was warm and friendly, and she never flinched at the idea of the disembodied heads. Instead she immediately dove into a hysterical improv with them and I just stood back and photographed.

LINDA ELLERBEE'S LAW: DO IT YOUR WAY, EVEN IF YOU'RE WRONG. YOU WILL PAY A PRICE FOR DOING IT YOUR WAY SOMETIMES, BUT WE ALL PAY PRICES IN LIFE. ONLY DEAD FISH SWIM WITH THE STREAM ALL THE TIME.

Lucia Rijker

Walking into the Wild Card Boxing Club in Los Angeles, I was almost knocked down by the smell of sweat alone, never mind being hit by anyone. There were twenty large men beating bags and one another, resulting in a perfume made from their sweat and the sweat of forty years' worth of men who came before them. The vibe in the gym was definitely Alpha Male. My assistant and I had never been so popular before. As the only two women there, surrounded by men pumped up with raging testosterone, we found it a little disconcerting and had to keep stepping outside, eagerly waiting for boxer Lucia Rijker to show up.

Eventually she arrived, an impressive figure in shades and a long black leather trench coat. Once inside, she switched on the light to the women's locker room, which had gone unused so far that day, and minutes later reemerged in her Everlast workout gear. The men responded to her completely differently than they had to us. Their respect for her was palpable. I tried to bond with her by commiserating about the smell, but she said she didn't notice it.

The thing I like best about Lucia Rijker is that she's not concerned with becoming a "great female athlete," but simply a great athlete. Period. I think that attitude, underscored by her never assuming that there are barriers specific to her gender, makes her push herself in ways that others may not. This Dutch welterweight, often referred to as "the most dangerous woman on Earth," has an undefeated record of 14–0 in the ring, including thirteen knockouts. In 1995 she fought in the New York Golden Gloves, the first time the tournament allowed women to compete, and she has participated in the only sanctioned mixed-gender boxing match on record.

LUCIA RIJKER'S LAW: DESTINY = KARMA

(CAUSE AND EFFECT)+ HARD WORK.

Lydia Lunch

It's notoriously difficult for people to decide whether they admire or revile what Lydia Lunch does. Often billed as a "confrontationalist" rather than as a poet or singer, she has stunned, alarmed, engaged, inspired, angered, and enraptured her audiences, sometimes all at once.

She fearlessly examines the norm and rips it to shreds, then tries to construct a philosophy that makes more sense to her. She turns a microscope on herself and her foibles, thereby encouraging others to do the same. Incest, an experience that has the potential to rob a woman of her sexual joy, is a subject Lydia uses to fuel her art. By fearlessly addressing such an uncomfortable, taboo subject she robs it of the power it might otherwise have to make a woman feel ashamed or shut down. She writes, "By the age of six, my sexual horizon was overstimulated by a father who had no control of his fantasies, natural tendencies, or criminal urges."

My assistant and I were greeted at Lydia's door by a guy she introduced as her "man slave," who then went into the kitchen to make us all some iced coffees. Lydia's home was beautifully decorated with heavy velvet curtains, candelabras, and dark wood furniture. However, when I took a step backward while focusing my camera and my foot went straight through a trapdoor in the floor that had been covered up by a small throw rug, it reminded me that I wasn't there shooting Martha Stewart.

LYDIA LUNCH'S LAW:
AS WOMEN, WE NEED TO
REALIZE OUR TRUE BEAUTY,
INCREDIBLE POWER, AND
UNIQUE ABILITIES. WE
MUST CONCENTRATE ON
OUR STRENGTHS, FIND OUR
VOICE, UNDERSTAND OUR
MISSION, ENCOURAGE
OUR DREAMS, AND FULFILL
OUR VISIONS. ONLY THE
INDIVIDUAL CAN SATISFY
HERSELF COMPLETELY.

Maggie Estep

For more than a decade Maggie Estep has been a treasure of the New York performance-art scene. Perhaps by now, though, she could more accurately be called a novelist, with two books out, *Diary of an Emotional Idiot* and *Soft Maniacs,* and another, *The Woman Who Ate the Sun,* forthcoming. She has performed and given readings throughout the United States and Europe at venues as diverse as Lollapalooza and Lincoln Center.

Born in New Jersey in 1963, Maggie traveled extensively as a child with her eccentric horse-trainer parents throughout the United States and France. "I was left," she says, "to run around naked and screaming and sticking my fingers in electrical sockets." That may account for the dark, schizophrenic sense of humor that's become her trademark. For example, she complains, "Dead people suck. You can't talk to them or give them the things you'd meant to give them." And of course, she is always making fun of herself and finding humor in her own shortcomings, as evidenced in her poem "I'm an Emotional Idiot."

I first became enamored of Maggie after I saw her rant and rave at Manhattan's Nuyorican Café about her miserable audition as a stripper years before and her misspent youth. The show prompted me to buy her album, *No More Mister Nice Girl,* which was loosely about life in the city, in particular as a single young woman, and was jam-packed with gems like "The Stupid Jerk I'm Obsessed With."

The day I was to photograph her, I arrived at her home carrying a fish. I proceeded to grease it with Vaseline, and then ask her to get into her tub with it. She never balked. Instead, she disappeared into the other room and reemerged with an armful of what turned out to be her precious collection of antique surgery tools. So we played with a greased-up fish and surgical tools for about two hours, comparing notes on what it was like for each of us to have been on her own since a young age and all the strange adventures that ensued.

I'm an Emotional Idiot
so get away from me.
I mean,
COME HERE.

Wait, no,
that's too close,
give me some space.
it's a big country,
there's plenty of room,
don't sit so close to me.
. . . .
God,
You're so cold.
I never know what you're thinking.
You're not very affectionate.

I mean,
you're clinging to me,
DON'T TOUCH ME,
what am I, your fucking cat?
Don't rub me like that.

Don't you have anything better to do
than sit there fawning over me?
. . . .
Move in with me.
we'll get a studio apartment together, save on rent,
well, wait, I mean, a one bedroom,
so we don't get in each other's hair or anything
or, well,
maybe a two bedroom
I'll have my own bedroom,
it's nothing personal
I just need to be alone sometimes,
you do understand,
don't you?

Hey, why are you acting distant?
. . . .
I'm an emotional idiot
so get away from me.
I mean,
MARRY ME.

MAGGIE ESTEP'S LAW: NO MATTER HOW SERIOUS A PLATE WE MAY GET THROWN, WE SHOULD NEVER LET IT MAKE US PUT A GUN TO OUR HEADS. AND WE SHOULD LAUGH. BECAUSE OTHERWISE WE'RE SCREWED.

Mary Karr

Articles about Mary Karr always refer to her as "wily," "scrappy," and "tough." And there's a lot of truth to that. Even though she's now a best-selling, well-respected author, she's still a tough Texas girl who has no qualms about telling you what she thinks.

MARY
KARR'S
LAW: LIKE
THE HIP-
HOP KIDS
SAY, "IT'S
ALL LOVE!"

She told me about walking out on a shoot with a photographer who asked her to pose next to a pattern in a stucco wall because he thought it looked like a penis. A makeup artist on another shoot made lewd comments about her body and pressed his crotch against her while she was sitting in the makeup chair and all five feet four inches of her threatened that if he didn't stop it she would "get out of this chair and kick your ass!"

For twenty years before she revealed the story of her childhood to the world in her best-selling memoir, *The Liar's Club*, Mary was a poet. As such, she couldn't have expected the kind of notoriety she has now, as the person often credited with having sparked the "memoir revival" of the 1990s.

Her follow-up to *The Liar's Club*, the recently released *Cherry*, continues the story into her adolescent years. In an interview I heard her do, she made a great point about how there is really no lighthearted libidinal language with which girls can talk about their sexuality. During the shoot we talked about all the various socially sanctioned outlets available to boys, who have *Playboy* and teen movies about "getting laid" and names for their private parts, which they talk about constantly. Girls don't have a comparable vocabulary, and Mary has set out to change that by telling her story in an unedited, funny, and poignant way that will likely ring true for her female readers.

When I read *The Liar's Club* and got to Mary's account of when the boy next door sexually attacked her when she was only seven, I thought "What a great use she's made of the space she's been given in the world." By writing *The Liar's Club*, Mary created a platform for herself from which her voice will forever resonate and she used it to take back some of the power this boy stole from her years ago.

Maybe her retelling the incident even changed that boy, now a grown man, if he recognized himself in the description. Regardless, I think it changed Mary and those who will read it and relate.

Nadine Strossen

Since the position of president of the American Civil Liberties Union (ACLU) is a nonpaying one, Nadine Strossen, who is serving as its first female president, continues to work as a professor of law at New York Law School. Among the many honors and awards bestowed on her as one of the country's great thinkers and shakers are her being named one of *Working Woman* magazine's "350 Women Who Changed the World, 1976–1996," and one of *Vanity Fair*'s "America's 200 Most Influential Women."

To head the ACLU is to court controversy. In 1995, with the release of her book *Defending Pornography: Free Speech, Sex, and the Fight for Women's Rights,* Nadine became the target for an onslaught of criticism from anti-pornography activists who thought she'd betrayed her feminist sisters.

In a radio interview Nadine elaborated on her views about pornography. "There's an argument that any sexual expression inherently undermines women's equality." But, she said, "it's a very difficult conflation between sex on the one hand and sexism on the other hand. There is much gender discrimination that doesn't involve sexual expression at all. Conversely, there's much sexual expression and conduct that is not gender discriminatory. There's a false equation between sexual expression and sexist harassment. The concentration on censoring pornography creates a dangerous diversion from issues of actual sexual discrimination."

She and I met at her apartment (on Manhattan's Upper West Side), which was only a couple of blocks from where I grew up. We were both familiar with many of the same neighborhood haunts and local characters, so the conversation flowed. Eventually we ended up talking about our families' backgrounds, which was when she told me this.

"I grew up constantly aware that the life options of both of my parents had been severely circumscribed as a result of pernicious stereotypes and discrimination. My father was imprisoned in the forced labor camp at Buchenwald, where he almost died before being liberated by the American armed forces. My mother, the daughter of immigrant parents with traditional views about a woman's role, was deflected from her decidedly nontraditional interests and values. Having always been painfully conscious that my parents had been prevented from pursuing their personal dreams and fulfilling their own potentials, due to societal stereotypes, I have seized every opportunity to conceptualize and realize my own vision of 'the good life' for myself as an individual—regardless of the norms or expectations of my society, community, family, or anyone else."

It is apparent from talking with her for two hours that Nadine is enthusiastic, unpretentious, funny, and secure enough in her own beliefs to invite conversation with people whose beliefs differ from hers.

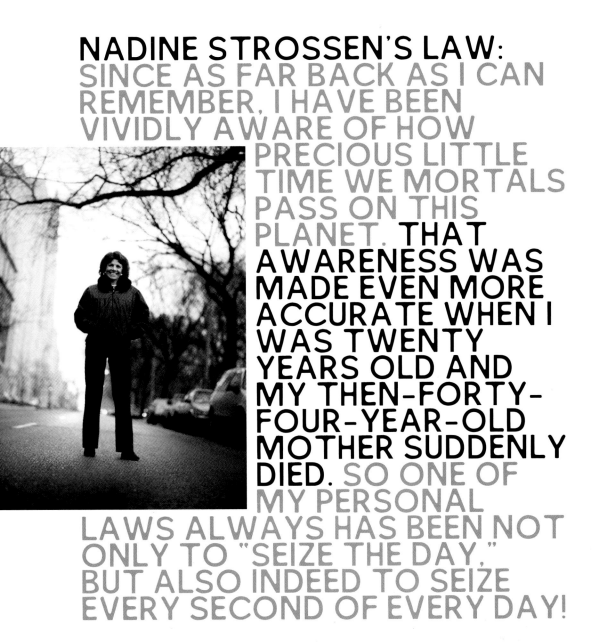

NADINE STROSSEN'S LAW: SINCE AS FAR BACK AS I CAN REMEMBER, I HAVE BEEN VIVIDLY AWARE OF HOW PRECIOUS LITTLE TIME WE MORTALS PASS ON THIS PLANET. **THAT AWARENESS WAS MADE EVEN MORE ACCURATE WHEN I WAS TWENTY YEARS OLD AND MY THEN-FORTY-FOUR-YEAR-OLD MOTHER SUDDENLY DIED.** SO ONE OF MY PERSONAL LAWS ALWAYS HAS BEEN NOT ONLY TO "SEIZE THE DAY," BUT ALSO INDEED TO SEIZE EVERY SECOND OF EVERY DAY!

Nell Merlino

Nell Merlino is a cofounder and the CEO of Count-Me-In for Women's Economic Independence, an organization that strives to create more opportunities for women starting their own businesses. Count-Me-In was formed in response to statistics showing that, for example, although women owned 38 percent of all U.S. businesses in 1998, only 1.7 percent of the venture capital funds distributed that year went to women.

Through fund-raising events and donations, money is raised from women and organizations and redistributed in the form of small-business loans to women with plans to start their own businesses. Donations start at as low as five dollars, making it possible for anyone to help. Rather than spending money on flashy ad campaigns, Count-Me-In relies on the grassroots approach of word-of-mouth and media attention to spread its name and cause. This allows all of the money raised to be channeled in the most effective ways to the women who need it.

"This is going to motivate millions of women and girls to do a simple task that will change economic history," Nell asserts.

In conjunction with the Ms. Foundation in 1993, Nell also created the now-annual, internationally celebrated Take Our Daughters to Work Day, meant to expose girls to more options for their futures and to promote their self-sufficiency and self-esteem. For her efforts on behalf of women, girls, and families, Nell was named Woman of the Year by *New Woman* magazine in 1993, and received the Fulbright Award for Outstanding Achievement in 1994.

Nell hired me to photograph a Count-Me-In fund-raising event a few years ago. The room was packed, and the overall vibe in the room was one of mutual support. Each woman, successful in various areas of business, was eager to share some of her good fortune for the common good.

NELL MERLINO'S LAW:
THINK BIGGER!
BE A MILLIONAIRE,
DON'T MARRY ONE.

Nora Dunn

Nora Dunn is best known for somehow making
her grotesque *Saturday Night Live* characters, like
one of the two Sweeney Sisters and Pat Stevens,
host of *The Pat Stevens Show,* very endearing.

More recently Nora has written a book called *Nobody's Rib,* which explores these characters (and others) further. She's also appeared in numerous films, one of her favorites, she tells me, being David O. Russell's antiwar epic, *Three Kings,* and has performed in the off-Broadway hit *The Vagina Monologues.*

I thought it was heroic when Nora refused to appear on the episode of *SNL* that was hosted by Andrew Dice Clay, whose homophobic and misogynist material she found offensive. "Women and homosexuals are the last bastion of this sort of 'humor,'" she tells me. "We are still asked to laugh at ourselves as vicious stereotypes drawn by people who are not particularly bright. People like Eminem aren't cutting edge. Their material is safe and acceptable. That is what is dangerous and shocking. That is why I did not agree with putting [Andrew Dice] Clay on the show."

Nora seems concerned with doing work she finds meaningful rather than reveling in celebrity. She says that she feels bad for those who take their celebrity as an opportunity to isolate themselves, because, when it's all said and done, they won't have enjoyed the time they spent working and making art.

NORA DUNN'S LAW: YOU HAVE TO LEARN TO LET GO OF SO MANY THINGS IN LIFE, LEARN TO ABSORB THE LOSSES. ART HELPS ME APPRECIATE ALL OF IT AND OF COURSE, THERE'S FOIE GRAS, CHERRY PIE, AND POT ROAST, TOO.

Pat Schroeder

Pat Schroeder became the first female member of the House of Representatives' Armed Services Committee in 1972, around the same time that its first African-American member was appointed. The chairman, disgruntled at this sign of the changing times, said, "That girl and that black are each worth about a half a regular member, so I'll give them one chair." And so, unbelievably, Pat Schroeder, congresswoman from Colorado, shared a single chair for her first two years of service, with Ron Dellums of California. In her remaining twenty-two years in Congress, and even after she left, she has been instrumental in making great strides for the equal representation of women and families in public policy by fighting for legalized abortion, increased funding for breast cancer research, passage of the Violence Against Women and Child Abuse Prevention Acts, the Federal Prohibition of Female Genital Mutilation Act, the Family and Medical Leave Act, and much more.

"My generation of women did not think you were meant to be a candidate," she says of her initial campaign for a seat in Congress. "You voted, you worked on a campaign, but you weren't a candidate." Her first twenty years in Congress seemed to reflect that thought, as she was one of very few female representatives. But in 1992, just after and in response to the Anita Hill/Clarence Thomas hearings, there was a sudden influx of women to Congress. "When the new class was getting sworn in," Pat says, "one of the old bulls came over and said, 'This place looks like a damned shopping mall thanks to people like you.' Even with 'the great influx,' only ten percent of the body was female. [Also] what shopping mall only has women?" And so I say "Thanks!" to Pat Schroeder and people like her.

PAT SCHROEDER'S LAW: LIFE IS NOT A DRESS REHEARSAL, IF YOU WANT TO TRY SOMETHING, JUST DO IT.

Paula Vogel

Paula Vogel won the Pulitzer Prize in 1998 for
her amazing play *How I Learned to Drive*.

"Every time I enter a theater or a movie or an art
gallery," Paula tells me, "I realize that by the time I
leave, I will be two hours closer to death. Now, each time
I sit down to write, I feel that urgency . . . to write something so compelling that people, when they leave the theater, will feel the two hours closer to death well spent."

Plays are not usually my favorite art form, so I was a little skeptical when I went to see *How I Learned to Drive* on a friend's recommendation. But it turned out to be the most cathartic experience I've ever had at any play or movie. Paula does a brilliant job of capturing the subtleties and nuances that exist between people in intense and difficult relationships. This play was an excellent example of her talent.

The story is narrated by a girl looking back on the incestuous yet loving relationship she'd had with her uncle throughout her childhood and on into adulthood. Writing can often lean toward summation and judgment; audiences like to identify and punish the bad and watch good clearly triumph over evil. But the reality is that life is a messy, unclear work in progress, in which emotions often conflict with reason and intellect. The main character in *How I Learned to Drive* has to come to terms with the love that she genuinely has for her uncle in light of the knowledge of how inappropriate and harmful his incestuous affection for her has been.

Paula and her partner live in a beautiful, sprawling home on an unassuming street in a quiet town, and on the day we meet we spend much of our time fussing over her newest acquisition, Moose, a beautiful little puppy whose presence reduces us both to cooing, laughing kids.

PAULA'S LAW: TO PARAPHRASE STELLA ADLER, THERE ARE THREE THINGS YOU NEED TO MAKE IT: 1. THE TENACITY OF A BULLDOG, 2. THE HIDE OF A RHINOCEROS, AND 3. A GOOD HOME TO COME HOME TO.

Sandra Bernhard

Sandra Bernhard's basic strength as a performer
lies in her complete fearlessness. She is uncon-
ventional in style and demeanor and has always
urged onlookers to "embrace their uniqueness."
She's provocative, hilarious, shocking, and always
very entertaining. She was as engaging to sit with
on a Sunday afternoon as she is to see perform.

Her career is totally defined by her personality and defies
categorization, steeped as it is in glamour, sex, comedy,
fantasy, a strong voice, and nerves of steel. In 1983 Sandra channeled all these things into her role as Marsha,
an obsessed fan, in Martin Scorsese's *King of Comedy*.
In the role, she yelled at, licked, tied up, serenaded, and
tortured two film legends, Robert De Niro and Jerry
Lewis, who would normally intimidate anyone acting
opposite them. It's that fearlessness, in addition to her
intelligence and perceptive wit, that makes her so good.

SANDRA BERNHARD'S LAW:

EVOLVE. EXPLORE. FUCK UP.

BUT NEVER BETRAY YOUR MUSE.

After years of defining herself as the eccentric, outrageous diva Miss Sandra Bernhard, it can be argued that she seems and looks better than ever before. In our conversations we talked a lot about her studies of Kabbalah and her relatively new role as mother to her little girl, who, at two, already has her mother's untamed red hair and inquisitive personality.

Sheryl
Swoopes

Sheryl Swoopes was raised by her single mother and taught to play basketball by her two brothers, whom she says were her role models growing up. Another figure she looked up to was Michael Jordan, so it's poignant that later, during her career with the WNBA, the press often referred to her as "the female Michael Jordan." (Jordan is also her son's name.)

Throughout high school and college Sheryl played on the girls' basketball teams and always ranked, if not *the* best, then among the top players. She was one of the first women signed to the WNBA in 1997, its first season, and three years later was named its MVP. She's also the first woman to have a sneaker, the Air Swoopes, named after her.

When I was in high school in the mid-1980s there was a girl named Lauren who was an incredible basketball player. She was the star of the girls' team, and during recess and after school, she was one of the best players— and usually the only girl—on the makeshift team the boys would throw together. I remember envying her talent so much and simultaneously wondering what on earth she would be able to do with it after she left school. As far as I knew, playing professional basketball, at least in America, wasn't an option for her, and even at the time, I knew that was criminal. This girl was a rare talent and she was forced to put a cap on her aspirations.

Sheryl brought her son and his nanny to our shoot. She was an impressive, stylish figure, gorgeous and incredibly tall in high-heeled boots. At first I think she was a little disappointed by my small photo studio setup. But once she realized how seriously I was taking these pictures and how creative I wanted to be with them (we tried a few different things, including a Madonna and child–type image with the basketball as "child"), she got into it, offering her own creative ideas.

141

SHERYL SWOOPES'S LAW: RESPECT YOUR TEAMMATES AND THE PLAYERS ON THE OPPOSING TEAM, FIRST AS PEOPLE, AND SECOND AS PLAYERS. ALWAYS TRY TO SHOW PEOPLE THE RESPECT YOU HOPE THEY'LL SHOW YOU. AND HELP THEM WITH THE THINGS THAT ARE HARDEST FOR THEM AS YOU WOULD HOPE THEY'D HELP YOU.

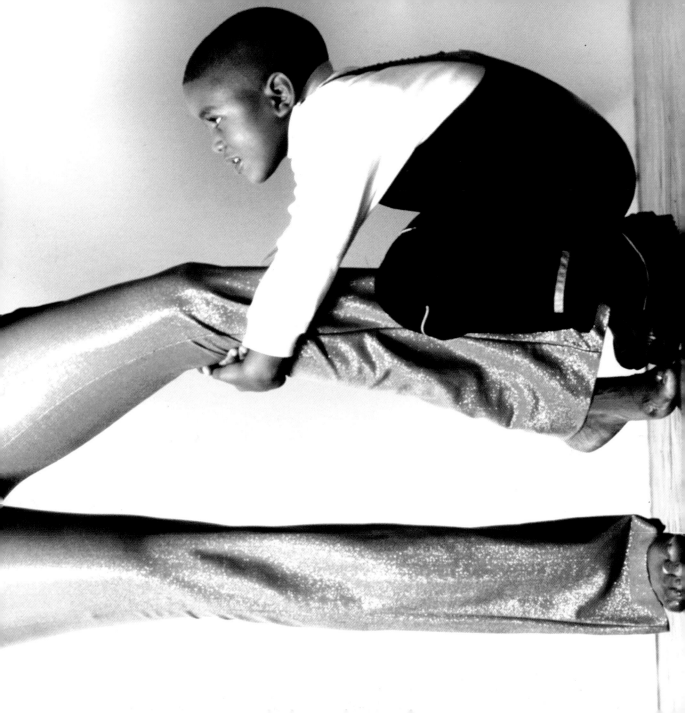

Sister Elaine Roulet

Everyone responds to Sister Elaine when she walks by. "Good morning . . . God bless you . . . Have a good day . . . I love you, Sister Elaine." And she responds in kind to every single person. Normally it wouldn't be surprising that people would address her respectfully, but the people who are showing her so much love are inmates at the Bedford Hills Women's Correctional Facility, in Westchester County, New York, and most of them are here because they've been convicted of violent crimes. The respect they have for her softens their faces, and there's a discernable change in the way that they stand around her. They really like her.

Sister Elaine is a funny, tough-talking, wisecracking woman ("To the holidays, all three hundred sixty five of them!" is her favorite Mae West quote) who began working at the prison in 1970. In 1980, she founded The Children's Center at Bedford Hills, a program designed to help the children of convicts to bond with their mothers and to educate the convicts about parenting. Statistics show that the majority of women in prison are there for crimes committed in response to domestic abuse. During their incarceration the women also receive drug rehabilitation treatment, where necessary, and education that they have missed, expanding their opportunities for employment upon their release and making a successful family life more likely on the outside.

Also in 1980, Sister Elaine founded Providence House, which offers housing for battered and homeless women and their children, and temporary housing for women released from prison. She realized that ghetto parishes were going unused and turned them into halfway homes. "I have always tried to be the 'Band-Aid Queen,'" Sister Elaine tells me. "Whenever I looked at the plight of children whose parents were incarcerated, I acted. Invariably I would hear, 'That's nothing but a Band-Aid approach.' I'd smile, knowing that Band-Aids call your attention to the fact that someone has been hurt. Band-Aids are public signs that someone is aware of your wound and cares."

SISTER ELAINE ROULET'S LAW: EVERY BANDIT NEEDS A POSSE. MY POSSE HAS ALWAYS INCLUDED SOME OF THE MOST UNEXPECTED PEOPLE, LIKE WARDENS, NUNS, CHILDREN, EX-OFFENDERS, INMATES, AND THE COMMUNITY. IF I WERE ALONE, I WOULD HAVE GIVEN UP YEARS AGO.

Susan Faludi

Susan Faludi is a creative, investigative thinker who has never been afraid to challenge status quo assumptions that promote a narrow view of the world. Released in 1991, her breakthrough book, *Backlash: The Undeclared War Against American Women,* became an essential ingredient in the education of enlightened women everywhere.

One of Susan's primary targets is the media, which she charges is morally irresponsible, reporting half-truths and ill-researched "facts" that perpetuate negative stereotypes about women. Recently, Faludi again sparked controversy by addressing the issue of gender identity in modern society, in *Stiffed: The Betrayal of the American Man.* This time she looks at what men do to define themselves in modern American culture where traditional demarcations between boys and men (the kind suggested, for example, by going to war), are no longer so clear.

SUSAN FALUDI'S LAW: PERSONAL PHILOSOPHIES ARE MEANT TO BE CHALLENGED . . . IDEALLY, EVERY DAY. A FEW YEARS AGO, I WAS VISITING WITH ONE OF MY FAVORITE PEOPLE, SWEDISH FEMINIST WRITER MARIA-PIA BOETHIUS, AND FOR SOME REASON THAT I NO LONGER REMEMBER, SHE BEGAN TO TELL ME ABOUT HER DAILY HABITS.

"WHEN I HAVE JUST WOKEN UP AND BEFORE I GET OUT OF BED," SHE TOLD ME, "I JUST LIE THERE AND QUESTION EVERYTHING." THIS IS AS GOOD A LAW TO LIVE BY AS ANY I KNOW.

Valerie Red-Horse

Traveling as a live model for Mattel's Pocahontas doll, released in conjunction with the animated movie *Pocahontas,* afforded Valerie Red-Horse the rare opportunity to talk with hundreds of people daily about the concerns of Native Americans.

When Valerie was growing up, Native Americans were never seen as the subjects of their own stories. Their parts in movies and television were limited to those of angry warriors (the bad guys), elder spiritual soothsayers, or virginal, innocent maidens. Their day-to-day experiences and concerns for the most part went untold. Angry about the dearth of good parts available to Native Americans, and dedicated to participating in work that accurately portrayed her people on film, Valerie Red-Horse started her own production company, Red-Horse Native Productions.

Naturally Native, the company's first major production, stars three Native American women and concerns itself with the issues of their daily lives at different ages. It is the first widely distributed film to be entirely funded by Native Americans. Valerie pleaded her case to the Mashantucket Pequot Tribe of Connecticut, who gladly funded the film, saying that the good that would come out of her efforts was more important than whether or not they would see a return on their investment.

VALERIE RED-HORSE'S LAW: THE IMAGE OF THE EAGLE IS A POWERFUL ONE FOR ME . . . ONE OF STRENGTH, OF THE ABILITY TO SOAR. I TRY TO CELEBRATE EACH DAY OF LIFE AND THANK THE LORD FOR EACH AND EVERY MOMENT.

In addition to producing and developing material, Valerie is also a writer. She was the first female Native American to be selected to participate in the prestigious Sundance Institute's Writer's Lab, which propelled her into numerous writing assignments. Involved in entertainment and as an investor on Wall Street, she remains committed to eroding stereotypes and providing opportunities for employment and self-expression for Native Americans.

As I loaded my camera to photograph Valerie in her hotel room in New York, I happened to look up and see her working at her laptop computer. The television was broadcasting the Home Shopping Network and she was dressed in a beautiful, traditional Native American leather jacket and turquoise necklace. I thought it was a really incongruous but interesting juxtaposition.

Waris Dirie

Waris Dirie grew up in a nomadic Somalian family, one of twelve children. When she was five—like her mother, aunts, cousins, and sisters—without anesthetic or preparation, she underwent a complete circumcision. After the procedure, her vagina was sewn up tightly and her legs were bound so that she couldn't walk (which might rip out the stitches). Waris survived this procedure, which results in death for one out of every four of the 2 million girls and women who are circumcised around the world each year (including two of Waris's sisters). Years later her father sold her as a teenage bride to a sixty-year-old man for five camels. Somehow this girl had a strong instinct for self-preservation, for she ended up running away, spending nine uncertain days and nights escaping through the desert and mountains. She managed to reach an uncle's house, where she stayed for a year, hiding her passport when he planned to return her.

Her uncle eventually moved, leaving her to live on her own. She started sweeping floors at a fast-food restaurant, and it was there that she was discovered by a photographer who helped her to launch what would become a very successful modeling career. She came to America, made money, and gained enough status to have the opportunity, as a United Nations ambassador, to educate people about the horrors of female genital mutilation.

WARIS DIRIE'S LAW: I BELIEVE THAT EVERYTHING IS POSSIBLE. THE DAY WILL ONLY GIVE WHAT YOU PUT INTO IT. IF YOU WAKE IN A MISERABLE MOOD AND DON'T DO ANYTHING TO CHANGE IT, THEN THE WHOLE DAY WILL BE MISERABLE. HOWEVER, IF YOU WAKE IN A POSITIVE MOOD AND USE IT PRODUCTIVELY, THEN THE WHOLE DAY WILL BE FULL OF CREATION AND SUCCESS.

For obvious reasons, the issue of sex has been a complex and daunting one for Waris. In interviews she says she has felt disgust for her body and imagines that others will feel the same. Plus there's chronic, extreme pain related to having sex, due to the irreparable damage done by her circumcision. Still, she found someone with whom she eventually felt safe enough to deal with this issue and with whom she has a beautiful child.

The morning I first spoke with her was the morning after she and her son escaped an electrical fire in their Brooklyn home. "I've never in my life woken up at four A.M. to get a glass of water," she told me. "We all have angels watching over us. Mine woke me up last night to get a glass of water and I discovered the living room was on fire." The morning after this experience she was positive and grateful to her guardian angels. She continues to be a survivor.

I recently called her to ask a question that's been on my mind since I read her story; does she currently have any relationship with her family? If so, is it at all a good one? She told me that she traveled back to Somalia in September of 2000 to visit her parents. "My trip," she said, "was a beautiful and heartfelt one. I was able to be underneath the stars with my mother and father and the rest of my entire family, like in the days of my childhood; the nomad way."

Epilogue

On Wednesday, July 25, 2001, I got a call, the likes of which
I've gotten five times in my life so far . . . someone was dead.
It had been over two months since I'd met the deadline for this book, some-
what on time, and I assumed that this story had been told. But on that
Wednesday morning, as I was headed out the door I got the news. Phoolan
Devi, the original Bandit Queen, whose legacy had been intricately entwined
with what I had thought and talked about for the two years prior, had been
shot and killed. Another strange and violent twist in a controversial life.

I felt oddly sad for someone I'd never met, which I saw as proof that
a person's legacy extends far beyond his or her physical body and can
shine brighter than the particulars of his or her short existence.
It's easy to find fault with Phoolan's actions. A life of revenge is not a
particularly enlightened one. But the atrocities that were committed
against her were probably more insidious because they were, sometimes subtly and sometimes overtly, made all right by the standards of
her society. Raped and beaten by her husband (her honor, and not his,
besmirched), raped by prison guards, undermined from birth because
of her gender; manifestations of cruel and unjust amorality firmly
ingrained in and accepted, to different degrees, in every society.
Anger has its place, but if it only inspires you to meet brute force with brute
force and not to find a way to improve what's wrong, anger is only half the story.
It's sad that much of Phoolan's story may have only gone as far as her justified
anger. Maybe her creativity came during her political career when she became
a heroine to many, championing particularly rights for women and the poor,
and inspiring those groups to persevere with her own story of rising above.

This Wednesday's revenge killing, done in retaliation for the killings alleged against Phoolan—for which she'd served eleven years in prison without a trial—continues the cycle of unenlightened brutality that plagued her life.

The effect she has had on people who, like me, are inspired by her refusal to accept abuse and suffering at the hands of traditions that are clearly amoral, is the way she added something positive to the world. Young girls in and around her home village still sing songs about the poor village girl who overcame and became an international phenomenon and perhaps they expect more for themselves than they would have otherwise.

Some of the Bandit Queens in My Life

I didn't want to let the opportunity pass me by to celebrate some of the Bandit Queens in my own life. These are women I know who inspire me, personally and artistically. They've all, at one time or another, proven themselves worthy of the titles "Bandit" and "Queen." They've all contributed positive things to the world, and I've benefited from knowing each of them. Some maybe you know, others you'll know someday, still others aren't in the business of making themselves known. But they're all wonderful, and we should all appreciate the ones who make our lives better.

Brooke Williams
photographer

Helene St. Claire
performing artist

Lily Wolf
musician, songwriter

Solveig Almaas
lucky lady

Bobbie Jean Fisher
Solveig's best friend

Cristina Campanella
multidisciplinary performer

Lisa Wisely
product development
manager, Blue Man Group

Taniya Holland
artist, photo rep

Jennifer Charles
singer for the Elysian Fields

Melissa Huffsmith-Roth
Slash Girl

Shannon O'Kelly White
PainfullyAware.com editrix

Sarah Silbert
singer, songwriter, editor

Jacquelyn Allegrezza
queen

Mary Smith
my mom

Kay Olsen
photographer

Yvonne Garrett
rock publicist

Janice Allegrezza
Ali's "cool" cousin

Andrea Lomanto
artist

Acknowledgments

Thank you so much, and all my love goes especially to:

Dean Williamson, Carrie Thornton, Steve Almaas (*Encontré la que yo buscaba*), Matt Verta-Ray, Lily Wolf, Parker Noon, Cristina Campanella, Ashley Jacobs, Taniya Holland, Kay Olsen, Gene Kliot (my guardian angel and patron saint), Mary Smith, Andre Smith, Shen, Meghan McDermott, the Caracino family, the Bauer family, the Allegrezza family, Doris Moreira, John Jaeger, Jeff Dworkin, Karen Gilhully, Daryl Ann Smith, Mark Steiner, Sarah Silbert, Rania at the Boho Studio, Michelle Yoo and Jerry at Non-Stock, Kristie Macris, Aurellio Valiere, Katherine Lee, Maia Stuart, Liz Margin, Helene St. Claire, Joanne Shwartz, Maria Buszeck, Paul Kolderie, Conrad Sanderson, Lisa Wisely, Bobby Fisher, Michele Quan, Mary Adams, Jon Heddigen, Carmine Coppola, Gigi Elmes, everyone at Lotus Minard Patton McIver, Babette Holland, Mayra Langdon-Riesman, George Wallach . . . and all of the women who were so kind and generous as to give me their time, energy, and thoughts for this book.

About the Author

As I sit writing this, I feel lucky. Playing music with my band has brought me to Porto, Portugal, which is also, coincidentally, where my mother's side of the family is from. It's incredibly beautiful here. At home, missing me, is the best man ever, and his incredible daughter, both of whom I love and miss more than anything. And after years of defining myself in various external ways—as a punk, a musician, a feminist, an artist—I finally feel I can start to integrate all those things and figure out who I actually am and exactly

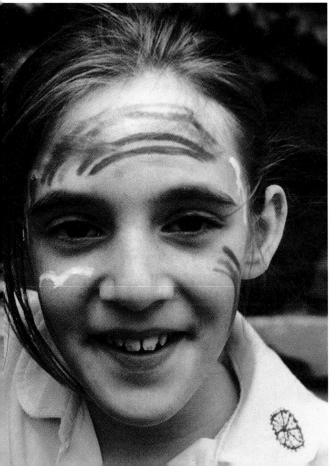

how I'd like to live my life. I've worked as a hospital cafeteria worker (cleaning puke off of patients' trays when they came back from their rooms), a strawberry picker (a punk-rock kid among a field of older, illegal immigrant men), a cartoonist, a graphic designer, a personal assistant to an eccentric filmmaker, an incompetent waiter, and a bartender in a rough Lower East Side dive (chronicled in my self-published photography book, *Sophie's Bar*), and I've finally come to the point where I can begin to survive on my art alone.

Mom was a nurse at NYU, whose tuition-assistance program for employees' family members allowed me to get my degree in photography virtually for free. Which was good, since from the age of sixteen, I've lived on my own and have long been in a position to have to support myself. I worked (and at a really low point, received welfare and food stamps) straight through college, which was in my hometown of New York City. Since the age of eighteen I've toured extensively with my own bands and others, and have gotten to document life on and behind stage in the music scene.

I've been fortunate enough so far to have had my photographs shown in group and solo shows in New York, Berlin, and San Francisco. If all goes well, the release of this book will find me working more and still living happily with Steve and Solveig Almaas in New York City . . . and, perhaps, also in Portugal.

MY LAW: BULLDOZE OVER YOUR FEARS. CHALLENGE THE LIMITATIONS YOU ASSUME APPLY TO YOU; PROCEED AS IF THEY DON'T EXIST. DARE TO GET ONSTAGE, OPEN YOUR MOUTH, SPEAK UP, WRITE A SONG, LOVE SOMEBODY WHO'S GOOD FOR YOU, EXPOSE YOUR TRUE SELF. DARE TO HAVE A DIF- FERENT OPINION, AND TO BE KIND IN THE FACE OF ADVERSITY. . . . JUST DARE.